HSP Science

Reading Support and Homework

Grade 2

Harcourt

SCHOOL PUBLISHERS

Visit *The Learning Site!*
www.harcourtschool.com

ISBN-13: 978-0-15-361023-3
ISBN-10: 0-15-361023-9

1 2 3 4 5 6 7 8 9 10   073   16 15 14 13 12 11 10 09 08 07

Contents

Chapter 1 — Living and Nonliving Things

Chapter 2 — Animals

Chapter 3 — Plants

Chapter 7 | Weather

Chapter 8 | The Solar System

Chapter 9 | Observing and Classifying Matter

Chapter 10 | Changes in Matter

Welcome to *Science!*

Find these things in your book.

1. What animal is on the cover of your book?

_____

2. How many chapters are in your book?

_____

3. Look on page 6. What word is in a yellow box?

_____

4. How many questions are on page 13?

_____

5. Look on page 29. What Inquiry Skill is shown?

_____

6. Look on page 38. Tell one Science Safety rule.

_____

Name _____

7. What is the first word in the glossary?

_____

8. What is the last word in the glossary?

_____

_____

9. Find a picture of something you like.
Tell about it.

_____

_____

Name _____

Date _____

Describe a Plant

Write to Inform–Describe

Look at a plant. Then write sentences that
describe the parts of the plant. Tell what each part
looks like and what it does. Use the outline to plan
your sentences.

Plant part	What it looks like	What it does

© Harcourt

Living and Nonliving Things

You can use these words together in sentences.

nonliving survive shelter nutrients living

Plants may need <u>nutrients</u> to <u>survive</u>.

A <u>shelter</u> may be made up of <u>nonliving</u> things.

Write a sentence that includes each word pair below. Use what you know about the words' meanings to help you.

1. living, shelter

_____

2. living, survive

_____

3. living, nonliving

_____

4. nonliving, nutrients

_____

© Harcourt

Name _____

Date _____

Lesson 1 - What Are Living and Nonliving Things?

1. **Inquiry Skill Practice—Classify**

One picture shows a living thing. One picture shows a nonliving thing. Label each picture. Tell how you know what kind of thing each is.

_____ _____

_____

_____

2. **Use Vocabulary**

Write the word that best completes each sentence.

A _____ thing does not need food, water, or gases.

| living |
| nonliving |

A _____ thing grows and changes. It needs food, water, and gases to live.

© Harcourt

Name _____

3. (Focus Skill) **Compare and Contrast**

Use this chart with the Lesson Review.

Living things	Nonliving things
A Living things _____, food and water.	**B** Nonliving things do not _____ food and water.
C Living things need _____.	**D** Nonliving things do not need _____.
E Living things make new _____ _____.	**F** _____ things can not make new things like themselves.

4. **Critical Thinking and Problem Solving**

A deer and a flower are both living things. They both need water to live. How do they get water in different ways?

_____

_____

_____

Name _____

Date _____

Lesson 2 - What Do Animals Need?

1. **Inquiry Skill Practice—Observe**

Observe the birds in this picture. Then fill in
the chart to tell how some birds get what
they need to survive.

How Some Birds Meet Their Needs	
food	
water	
shelter	

2. **Use Vocabulary**

Match the word to its meaning.

survive •   • a safe place to live

shelter •   • stay alive

Name _____

3. ⭐ Focus Skill **Main Idea and Details**

Use this chart with the Lesson Review.

Main Idea and Details

Animals need many things to survive.

Animals need space to move around.	Animals need **Ⓐ** _____ to eat.	Animals need **Ⓑ** _____ to drink.	Animals need **Ⓒ** _____ to stay safe.	Animals need **Ⓓ** _____ from air or water.

4. **Critical Thinking and Problem Solving**

How do a bear and a fish get oxygen, shelter, and food in different ways?

_____

_____

_____

© Harcourt

Name _____

Date _____

Lesson 3 - What Do Plants Need?

1. **Inquiry Skill Practice—Predict**

Read about each plant, and predict what will happen to it.

Plant 1

Plant 2

Plant 1 gets enough water. It is in a sunny spot in the garden.

Plant 2 does not get enough water. It does not get enough sun in the garden.

Prediction _____

_____

_____

Prediction _____

_____

_____

2. **Use Vocabulary**

Match the word to its meaning.

• different amounts of water

nutrients •

• minerals

© Harcourt

Name _____

3. (Focus Skill) Main Idea and Details

Use this chart with the Lesson Review.

Main Idea and Details

```
┌─────────────────────────────────────────┐
│   Plants need many things to grow        │
│          and stay healthy.               │
└─────────────────────────────────────────┘
```

Plants need water, **A** _____, and _____ to make food.	Plants need **B** _____ from the soil.	Plants need **C** _____ to grow bigger.

4. Critical Thinking and Problem Solving

Suppose you had a plant that had gotten too big for its pot. What could you do to help it grow and stay healthy?

_____

_____

Animals

The following words are related. They all tell about frogs.

tadpole   jump   amphibian   swim

A <u>tadpole</u> is a young frog. An <u>amphibian</u> is the type of animal a frog is. <u>Jump</u> and <u>swim</u> tell how frogs move.

Write a word from the box that tells about it in some way. You may use some words for more than one animal group. Then write two more words that can tell about it.

1. mammal

_____

_____

_____

2. bird

_____

_____

_____

3. reptile

_____

_____

_____

scales

feathers

lungs

© Harcourt

Name _____

Date _____

Lesson 1 - What Are Mammals and Birds?

1. **Inquiry Skill Practice–Compare**

One picture shows a mammal. The other shows a bird. Label each picture. Tell how you know what each animal is.

_____   _____

_____

_____

_____

2. **Use Vocabulary**

Write the word that best completes each sentence.

Mammals	Birds

_____ lay eggs.

_____ give birth to live young.

Name _____

3. Focus Skill | Compare and Contrast

Use this chart with the Lesson Review.

Mammals and Birds

alike   **different**

| Both have body coverings. |

| Mammals have fur or **A** _____. |
| Birds have **B** _____. |

| Both have young. |

| Mammals have **C** _____. |
| Birds lay **D** _____. |

4. Critical Thinking and Problem Solving

Suppose you are a scientist. How would you group these animals? Explain why.

 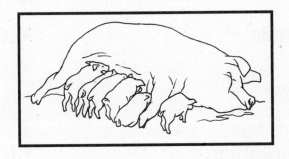

_____

_____

© Harcourt

Name _____

Date _____

Lesson 2 - What Are Reptiles, Amphibians, and Fish?

1. **Inquiry Skill Practice–Classify**

Classify these animals into three groups. List the animals in each group.

toad   **alligator**   **angelfish**   **lizard**   **shark**   **frog**

Reptiles	Amphibians	Fish

2. **Use Vocabulary**

Match the word to the words that tell about it.

reptile •

    • It lives in the water when it is young. It lives on land when it is an adult.

amphibian •

    • It lives in water and takes in oxygen through gills.

fish •

    • Its skin is rough, dry, and covered with scales.

Name _____

3. (Focus Skill) **Compare and Contrast**

Use this chart with the Lesson Review.

> **Reptiles, Amphibians, Fish**

alike	different
All have body coverings.	Reptiles have dry, scaly skin. Amphibians have **A** _____, wet skin. Fish have **B** _____.
All have a place to live.	Reptiles live on land or in **C** _____. Young amphibians live **D** _____. Adult amphibians live **E** _____. Fish live **F** _____.

4. **Critical Thinking and Problem Solving**

A turtle is the only reptile with a shell. How does a shell help protect a turtle?

_____

_____

_____

Name _____

Date _____

Lesson 3 - What Are Some Animal Life Cycles?

1. **Inquiry Skill Practice—Sequence**

Numbers show the order in which things happened. Write 1, 2, and 3 below the correct pictures to show the sequence of events.

_____ _____ _____

2. **Use Vocabulary**

Match the picture to the word or words that describe it.

life cycle •

tadpole •

Name _____

3. Focus Skill **Sequence**

Use this chart with the Lesson Review.

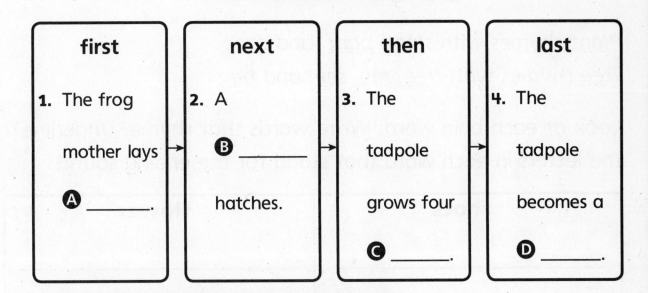

Frog Life Cycle

first	next	then	last
1. The frog mother lays **A** _____.	2. A **B** _____ hatches.	3. The tadpole grows four **C** _____.	4. The tadpole becomes a **D** _____.

4. **Critical Thinking and Problem Solving**

How is the life cycle of an amphibian different from the life cycle of a mammal?

_____

_____

_____

_____

Name _____

Date _____

Plants

When two words rhyme, they have the same ending sounds, but different beginning sounds. For example:

Pl<u>ant</u> rhymes with *sl<u>ant</u>*, *p<u>ant</u>*, and *c<u>an't</u>*.
Tr<u>ee</u> rhymes with *fr<u>ee</u>*, *m<u>e</u>*, *s<u>ee</u>*, and *b<u>e</u>*.

Look at each bold word. Write words that rhyme. Underline the letters in each word that stand for the ending sound.

roots	**flower**
_____	_____
_____	_____
shrub	**trunk**
_____	_____
_____	_____

Write a sentence that uses at least three words from the chart. Include one word that has to do with plants.

_____

_____

© Harcourt

Name _____

Date _____

Lesson 1 - What Are the Parts of a Plant?

1. **Inquiry Skill Practice–Observe**

Plant A got sunlight, air, water, and nutrients.
Plant B did not. Observe both plants and tell
about the parts of each plant.

Plant A   Plant B

Observations: _____   Observations: _____

_____   _____

_____   _____

2. **Use Vocabulary**

Match the term to the part
of the plant it describes.

roots •

stem •

leaves •

flower •

© Harcourt

Name _____

3. Focus Skill ▐ **Main Idea and Details** ▌

Use this chart with the Lesson Review.

Main Idea and Details

┌───┐
│ Each part of a plant helps the plant get   │
│ the things it needs to live.   │
└───┘

┌──────────────┐ ┌──────────────┐ ┌──────────────┐ ┌──────────────┐
│ Roots take in│ │ A **B** _____│ │ Leaves make │ │ **D** _____ │
│   │ │ carries water│ │   │ │   │
│ **A** _____ │ │ to the leaves.│ │ **C** _____ │ │ help plants │
│ and nutrients│ │   │ │ for the plant.│ │ make new   │
│ from soil.   │ │   │ │   │ │ plants.   │
└──────────────┘ └──────────────┘ └──────────────┘ └──────────────┘

4. ▐ **Critical Thinking and Problem Solving** ▌

Observe the plant. What might
happen to it? Why?

_____

_____

_____

Name _____

Date _____

Lesson 2 - How Do Plants Differ?

1. **Inquiry Skill Practice–Classify**

Use the chart to classify the leaves into three groups. List the trees the leaves come from in each group.

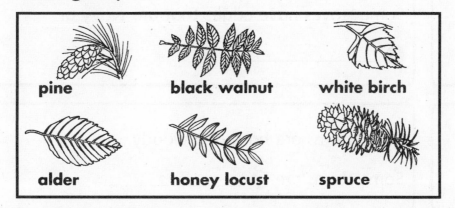

pine   black walnut   white birch

alder   honey locust   spruce

One Large Leaf	Many Small Leaflets	Needles

2. **Use Vocabulary**

Match the term to the sentences that tell about it.

shrub •

     • It is hard and woody. It is the main stem of a tree.

trunk •

     • It has many woody stems. It is also called a bush.

© Harcourt

Use with pages 124–131.   (page 1 of 2)   **Reading Support and Homework**   **RS 21**

Name _____

3. (Focus Skill) Compare and Contrast

Use this chart with the Lesson Review.

Plants

alike	different
Plants have leaves.	Some leaves have smooth edges. Some leaves have edges that are wavy or **A** _____.
Plants have stems.	Some stems are hard and woody. Some stems are **B** _____.
Plants have roots.	Some plants have one **C** _____ root. Some plants have many **D** _____ roots.

4. Critical Thinking and Problem Solving

Suppose you and a friend want to find out whether two plants are the same kind of plant. What could you do to find out?

_____

_____

Name _____

Date _____

Lesson 3 - What Are Some Plant Life Cycles?

1. **Inquiry Skill Practice–Communicate**

Read about how a plant is growing. Then draw pictures to communicate what is happening.

_____ _____ _____

_____ _____ _____

_____ _____ _____

2. **Use Vocabulary**

Write the term that best completes each sentence.

life cycle **germinate**

Seeds need oxygen, water, and warmth to _____.

All the stages of a plant's life make up its _____.

Name _____

3. ⭐ (Focus Skill) **Sequence**

Use this chart with the Lesson Review.

┌─────────────────────────────────────┐
│   **Life Cycle of a Bean Plant**   │
└─────────────────────────────────────┘

| A bean seed germinates. First, the Ⓐ _____ grows down. | → | Next, the Ⓑ _____ breaks the ground. | → | Then, more leaves and stems grow. The plant also makes Ⓒ _____ and seeds. | → | Last, a new Ⓓ _____ begins. |

4. **Critical Thinking and Problem Solving**

What would happen if maple trees stopped making seeds?

_____

_____

Name _____

Date _____

Write to Describe

A. Draw a plant or an animal that lives at each level of the rain forest.

In the treetops

_____

_____

In the middle of the branches

_____

_____

_____

On the ground

_____

_____

_____

B. Write describing words next to each picture you drew.

Living Things in Their Environments

You can use these words together in many ways.

habitat   adapt   rain forest   grassland   desert
ocean   pond   food chain   environment

An animal must <u>adapt</u> to its <u>environment</u>.

An <u>ocean</u> is much bigger than a <u>pond</u>.

Read each phrase below. Draw a picture that shows its meaning.

a <u>rain forest habitat</u>	an <u>ocean</u> <u>food chain</u>
an animal <u>has adapted</u> to the <u>desert</u>	**a <u>grassland</u> <u>habitat</u>**

© Harcourt

Name _____

Date _____

Lesson 1 - What Is an Environment?

1. **Inquiry Skill Practice–Make a Model**

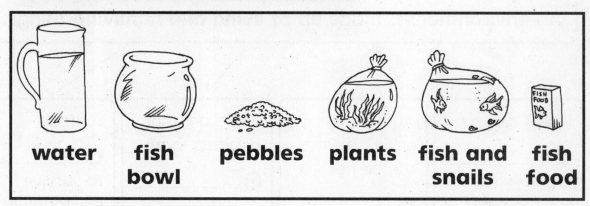

water **fish bowl** **pebbles** **plants** **fish and snails** **fish food**

Draw a picture to show how these materials can be used to make a model of how living things get energy.

2. **Use Vocabulary**

Match the word to the words that tell about it.

environment •

habitat •

adapt •

• a place where animals get the food, water, and shelter they need to live

• all the living and nonliving things in a place

• to change in order to live in an environment

Name _____

3. (Focus Skill) Main Idea and Details

Use this chart with the Lesson Review.

Main Idea and Details

An environment is made up of living and nonliving things.

| Plants and **A** _____ live in environments. | An environment can be hot, **B** _____, **C** _____, or dry. | There are many habitats in an **D** _____. | Animals **E** _____ to survive in an environment. |

4. Critical Thinking and Problem Solving

Otters have fur and webbed feet. What can you tell about an otter's habitat?

_____

_____

_____

Name _____

Date _____

Lesson 2 - How Do Living Things Survive in Different Places?

1. **Inquiry Skill Practice–Infer**

This picture shows giraffes in a grassland. How have giraffes adapted to help them survive?

_____

_____

_____

2. **Use Vocabulary**

Write the word that best completes each sentence.

tundra	rain forest	pond

A _____ is a small freshwater environment.

A _____ is a wet environment.

A _____ is cold and snowy.

© Harcourt

Name _____

3. (Focus Skill) **Main Idea and Details**

Use this chart with the Lesson Review.

Main Idea and Details

Plants and animals have adapted to living in many environments.

| A cactus in the desert can store water. | Grassland animals travel **A** _____. | Animals that live in a tundra have thick **B** _____. | Some ocean animals change colors to **C** _____. | Plants in a pond grow where they can get **D** _____. |

4. **Critical Thinking and Problem Solving**

How are grassland and tundra environments alike and different?

_____

_____

_____

_____

Lesson 3 - What Are Food Chains and Food Webs?

1. **Inquiry Skill Practice–Communicate**

These pictures show a food chain. Write
sentences that tell about the food chain.

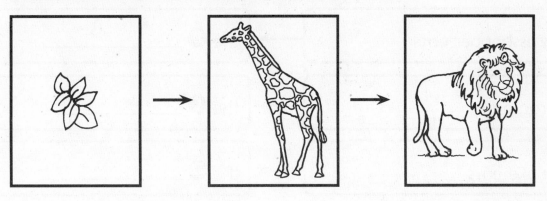

_____

_____

2. **Use Vocabulary**

Write the word that best completes
each sentence.

food web	food chain

A _____ shows the order in which animals eat
plants and other animals.

A _____ shows how food chains are connected.

© Harcourt

Name _____

3. 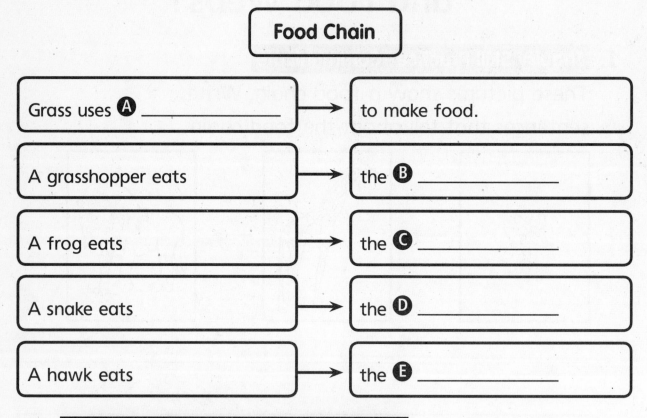 Focus Skill Sequence

Use this chart with the Lesson Review.

Food Chain

Grass uses **Ⓐ** _____	→ to make food.
A grasshopper eats	→ the **Ⓑ** _____
A frog eats	→ the **Ⓒ** _____
A snake eats	→ the **Ⓓ** _____
A hawk eats	→ the **Ⓔ** _____

4. Critical Thinking and Problem Solving

Think about the food chain above. What would happen if many grasshoppers got sick and died?

_____

_____

_____

© Harcourt

Name _____

Date _____

Tell a Recycling Story

Write to Express–Narrative

Suppose you are something that will be reused in a recycling project. Write a story that tells what you were first used for, how you were recycled, and what you are used for now. Use the story map below to help you plan your story.

What are you?
What were you used for first?
How were you recycled?
What are you used for now?

© Harcourt

Exploring Earth's Surface

<u>Exploring</u> is another way to say <u>finding out about</u>.
<u>Earth</u> is another way to say <u>our planet</u>. So <u>exploring Earth</u> is
another way to say <u>finding out about our planet</u>.

Match the words to the phrases.

erosion•   • dirt

earthquake•   • shaking ground

boulder•   • wearing away

soil•   • big rock

Rewrite the sentences with different words.

1. A lot of <u>dirt</u> was lost due to <u>wearing away</u> of
the land.

_____

2. The <u>shaking ground</u> moved the <u>big rock</u>.

_____

© Harcourt

Name _____

Date _____

Lesson 1 - What Changes Earth's Surface?

1. Inquiry Skill Practice-Observe

The pictures show how a rock changed over time. Observe them carefully. Then write a caption for each picture.

_____ _____ _____

_____ _____ _____

_____ _____ _____

2. Use Vocabulary

Match the term to the words that tell about it.

erosion •   • wind and water break down rock into smaller pieces

weathering •   • a place where lava comes out of the ground

earthquake •   • wind or moving water moves sand and small rocks

volcano •   • a shaking of Earth's surface

© Harcourt

Name _____

3. 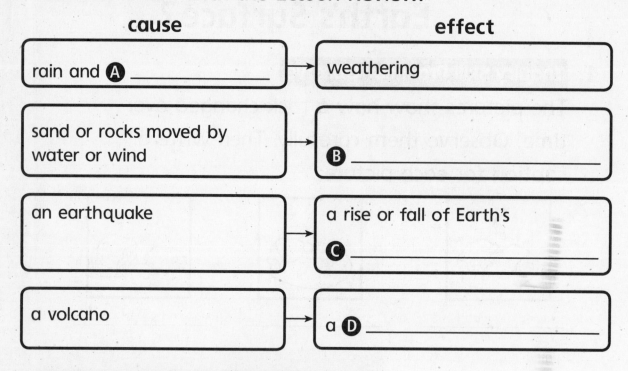 Focus Skill Cause and Effect

Use this chart with the Lesson Review.

cause	effect

rain and **A** _____	→	weathering
sand or rocks moved by water or wind	→	**B** _____
an earthquake	→	a rise or fall of Earth's **C** _____
a volcano	→	a **D** _____

4. Critical Thinking and Problem Solving

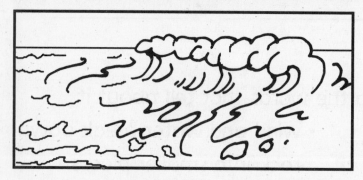

How can waves at a beach cause erosion?

_____

_____

_____

Name _____

Date _____

Lesson 2 - What Are Rocks, Sand, and Soil?

1. `Inquiry Skill Practice–Draw Conclusions`

Each picture shows a tree. The caption tells about soil where the tree grows.

Black Spruce Tree   Red Oak Tree   Sand Pine Tree

wet soil   rocky soil   sandy soil

What conclusions can you draw from the pictures and captions?

_____

2. `Use Vocabulary`

Match the term to the words that tell about it.

mineral •

      • bits of rock mixed with matter that was once living

boulder •

      • solid matter that makes up rocks

soil •

      • a very large rock

Name _____

3. (Focus Skill) Compare and Contrast

Use this chart with the Lesson Review.

$$\boxed{\textbf{Rocks}}$$

alike

> They are pieces of
> Ⓐ _____ crust.

> They are made up of
> Ⓑ _____.

different

> They can be different colors.

> They can be large or
> Ⓒ _____.

> They can be rough or
> Ⓓ _____.

4. Critical Thinking and Problem Solving

What can you tell about a plant that grows in soil that holds little water?

_____

_____

Name _____

Date _____

Lesson 3 - What Can We Learn from Fossils?

1. **Inquiry Skill Practice–Communicate**

Suppose you are a scientist. You uncover three fossils. Communicate what each one is and whether it is from a plant or an animal.

_____   _____

2. **Use Vocabulary**

Write the term that best completes each sentence.

dinosaur	fossil	extinct

A _____ is what is left of an animal or a plant that lived long ago.

A _____ is an animal that lived on Earth millions of years ago.

Animals that died out are _____.

Name _____

3. Focus Skill **Sequence**

Use this chart with the Lesson Review.

How a Trilobite Fossil Forms

First, a trilobite	Next, its	Last, the mud, the
A _____. Mud and sand covered it.	**B** _____ parts rotted away and its **C** _____ parts remained.	sand, and the hard parts of the trilobite slowly turned to **D** _____.

4. **Critical Thinking and Problem Solving**

What can you tell from this fossil about where the animal lived and how it moved? How could you learn more about the extinct animal?

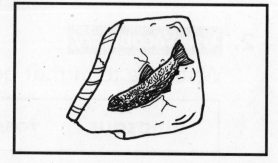

_____

_____

_____

_____

Name _____

Date _____

Natural Resources

Look at the words below. All of them have to do with natural resources. But some are words for <u>nouns</u>. Others are words for <u>actions</u>.

nouns		actions	
animals	trash	save	reduce
water	air	protect	help

I do not waste <u>water</u>.   I <u>protect</u> natural resources.

Draw a picture to go with each word below. Then circle the <u>nouns</u>. Underline the <u>actions</u>.

pollution	reuse
recycle	**resource**

Name _____

Date _____

Lesson 1 - How Can People Use Natural Resources?

1. **Inquiry Skill Practice–Draw Conclusions**

Draw conclusions about the way this family uses plants.

_____

_____

2. **Use Vocabulary**

Write the term that best completes each sentence.

natural resource	resource

Anything that people use to meet their needs is

a _____.

Trees are a _____ because they come from nature and are used in many ways.

Name _____

3. **Main Idea and Details**

Use this chart with the Lesson Review.

Main Idea and Details

People use natural resources to meet their needs.

| People breathe **A** _____ . | People use **B** _____ to clean. | People use **C** _____ to get metal. | People use **D** _____ to make bricks to build with. | People use **E** _____ to make clothes and paper. |

4. **Critical Thinking and Problem Solving**

How are these things alike?

_____

_____

_____

Name _____

Date _____

Lesson 2 - How Can People Harm Natural Resources?

1. **Inquiry Skill Practice–Observe**

Observe this park. Mark an X on all the things that people can clean up.

2. **Use Vocabulary**

Match the word to the picture that shows its meaning.

pollution •

•

•

Name _____

3. Focus Skill **Cause and Effect**

Use this chart with the Lesson Review.

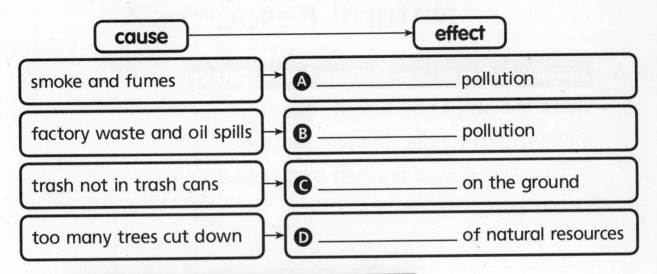

cause	→	effect
smoke and fumes	→	Ⓐ _____ pollution
factory waste and oil spills	→	Ⓑ _____ pollution
trash not in trash cans	→	Ⓒ _____ on the ground
too many trees cut down	→	Ⓓ _____ of natural resources

4. **Critical Thinking and Problem Solving**

Suppose you wanted to build a house on this land and still protect its natural resources. What could you do? How would it protect the natural resources?

_____

_____

_____

© Harcourt

Name _____

Date _____

Lesson 3 - How Can People Protect Natural Resources?

1. **Inquiry Skill Practice–Plan an Investigation**

Write the steps you would take to make a bird feeder. Draw a picture to show how your finished bird feeder would look.

_____

_____

_____

2. **Use Vocabulary**

Write the word that best completes each sentence.

endangered	reuse	reduce	recycle

You can _____ a food jar by storing buttons or marbles in it.

You can _____ things made of glass and paper so that they can be used to make new things.

People help _____ air pollution by riding a bike.

People can help _____ animals.

© Harcourt

Name _____

3. (Focus Skill) **Cause and Effect**

Use this chart with the Lesson Review.

| cause | → | effect |

People reuse things. → They save **A** _____.

They make less **B** _____.

People recycle things. → They use old things to make **C** _____ things.

They make less **D** _____.

4. **Critical Thinking and Problem Solving**

Suppose you are on your town council. What laws would you pass to protect the natural resources of your community?

_____

_____

_____

_____

Name _____

Date _____

Describe a Planet

Write to Inform–Description

Choose a planet other than Earth from our solar system.
Write a paragraph that describes the planet. Use a
children's reference book and the outline below to help
you plan your paragraph.

Planet name	Place in the solar system
Size and color of the planet	**Hot or cold**
Other interesting facts about the planet	

Weather

Context clues can help you understand the meaning of a new word. In the sentences below, <u>time of year</u> helps you understand what a <u>season</u> is:

Spring is Kelly's favorite <u>season</u>. She says it is a beautiful <u>time of year</u>.

Find context clues to figure out the meaning of each underlined word. Draw a line under the clues. Circle the letter next to the words that best complete the sentence.

1. It did not take long for the puddle to <u>evaporate</u>. It seemed to disappear under the hot sun. To <u>evaporate</u> is _____.

   A to get bigger   **C** to go into the air

   B to get cold   **D** to turn to liquid

2. We wanted to know how hot it was outside, so we found out the <u>temperature</u>. <u>Temperature</u> is _____.

   A how fast the air is moving

   B the amount of rain

   C a tool for measuring

   D how warm the air is

Name _____

Date _____

Lesson 1 - How Does Weather Change?

1. **Inquiry Skill Practice–Observe**

How did the weather change from morning to afternoon? What changes do you observe?

morning

afternoon

_____

_____

_____

2. **Use Vocabulary**

Write the term that best completes each sentence.

seasons	weather pattern

A weather change that repeats is a _____.

There are four _____ in a year.

Name _____

3. ⭐ **Focus Skill** | **Sequence**

Use this chart with the Lesson Review.

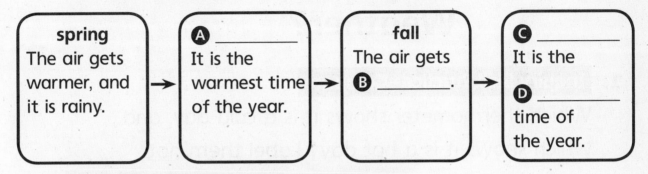

| spring
The air gets warmer, and it is rainy. | **A** _____
It is the warmest time of the year. | fall
The air gets **B** _____. | **C** _____
It is the **D** _____ time of the year. |

4. **Critical Thinking and Problem Solving**

Suppose a friend sent you these pictures but did not tell you when they were taken. Use the clues in each picture to identify the season, and write it in the blank.

_____ _____ _____ _____

Name _____

Date _____

Lesson 2 - Why Do We Measure Weather?

1. **Inquiry Skill Practice–Compare**

Which thermometer shows it is a cold day, and
which shows it is a hot day? Label them <u>hot</u>
and <u>cold</u>. Tell how you know.

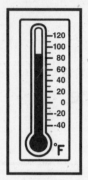 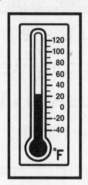

_____ _____

_____

_____

2. **Use Vocabulary**

Write the word that best completes each sentence.

precipitation	**thermometer**

Rain and sleet are two kinds of _____.

A _____ measures how hot or cold the air is.

Name _____

3. ⭐(Focus Skill) ■ **Main Idea and Details** ■

Use this chart with the Lesson Review.

Main Idea and Details

┌─────────────────────────────┐
│ **Scientists use tools**   │
│ **to measure weather.**   │
└─────────────────────────────┘

┌──────────────┐ ┌──────────────┐ ┌──────────────┐ ┌──────────────┐
│ A **A** _____ │ │ An anemometer│ │ A **C** _____ │ │ A   │
│   │ │ measures the │ │   │ │   │
│ _____   │ │ speed of the │ │ _____   │ │ **D** _____   │
│ measures how │ │ **B** _____   │ │ shows the   │ │ measures the │
│ much rain   │ │   │ │ direction of │ │ temperature of│
│ falls.   │ │   │ │ the wind.   │ │ the air.   │
└──────────────┘ └──────────────┘ └──────────────┘ └──────────────┘

4. ■ **Critical Thinking and Problem Solving** ■

Look at these pictures. Which one do you
think shows the best wind for flying a kite?
Tell why.

_____

_____

_____

Name _____

Date _____

Lesson 3 - What Is the Water Cycle?

1. **Inquiry Skill Practice–Infer**

What happened to the puddle of water? Infer
what caused the change.

_____

_____

_____

2. **Use Vocabulary**

Match each word to the words that tell about it.

water cycle •   • Heat changes water to a gas.

drought •   • Water vapor cools and changes into
water droplets.

condenses •   • This is all the movements of water
between Earth's surface and the air.

evaporates •   • This is a long period with little or
no rain.

© Harcourt

RS 54   Reading Support and Homework   (page 1 of 2)   Use with pages 292–301.

Name _____

3. ⭐ (Focus Skill) **Cause and Effect**

Use this chart with the Lesson Review.

cause	effect
The sun's heat warms water. →	Water **A** _____.
Water vapor meets cool air. →	Water vapor **B** _____.
Too little rain falls. →	There is a **C** _____.
Too much rain falls. →	There is a **D** _____.

4. **Critical Thinking and Problem Solving**

Suppose you are playing outside. You start to see dark clouds. You hear thunder. What do you think will happen? What should you do?

_____

_____

_____

The Solar System

A word family is made up of words with the same base. Each group below shows words from the same family.

sunny	moved
sunshine	movement
sunburn	moving

Use each base word below to make new words. For some words you have to drop the final e before adding an ending.

1. season Add –al, –able. _____ _____	**3. rotate** Add –ing, –ion. _____ _____
2. moon Add –s, –lit, –less. _____ _____	**4. orbit** Add –ed, –ing, –s. _____ _____

Choose two new words you made above. Use their bases to figure out what they mean. Then use each one in a sentence.

_____

_____

© Harcourt

Lesson 1 - What Are Stars and Planets?

1. **Inquiry Skill Practice–Infer**

Look at these pictures. Infer why it is harder for the boy in the city to see the stars at night.

_____

_____

2. **Use Vocabulary**

Match each word to the words that tell about it.

solar system •   • a large ball of rock or gas that moves around the sun

planet •   • a path around something

orbit •   • a group of stars that forms a pattern

star •   • the sun, the planets, and the planets' moons

constellation •   • a huge ball of hot gases

© Harcourt

Name _____

3. 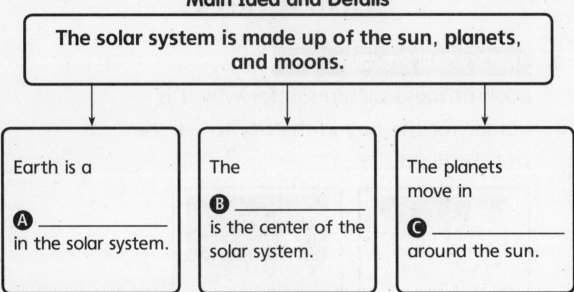 Focus Skill **Main Idea and Details**

Use this chart with the Lesson Review.

Main Idea and Details

The solar system is made up of the sun, planets, and moons.

| Earth is a **A** _____ in the solar system. | The **B** _____ is the center of the solar system. | The planets move in **C** _____ around the sun. |

4. **Critical Thinking and Problem Solving**

Mercury is the planet closest to the sun. Neptune is the planet farthest away from the sun. Which planet do you think takes longer to orbit the sun? Why?

_____

_____

_____

© Harcourt

Name _____

Date _____

Lesson 2 - What Causes Day and Night?

1. **Inquiry Skill Practice–Observe**

Observe the shadow at different times during the day. Write your observations below.

     morning   **noon**   **evening**

_____

_____

_____

2. **Use Vocabulary**

Match the word to the words that tell about it.

           • moves back and forth quickly

rotates •   • moves up and down slowly

           • spins around and around

Name _____

3. 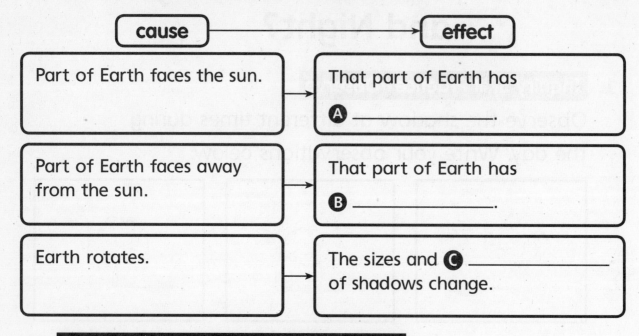 **Cause and Effect**

Use this chart with the Lesson Review.

| cause | → | effect |

Part of Earth faces the sun. → That part of Earth has Ⓐ _____.

Part of Earth faces away from the sun. → That part of Earth has Ⓑ _____.

Earth rotates. → The sizes and Ⓒ _____ of shadows change.

4. **Critical Thinking and Problem Solving**

How do you know when it is morning for people who live on the other side of Earth from you? Explain.

_____

_____

_____

_____

Name _____

Date _____

Lesson 3 - Why Does the Moon Seem to Change?

1. **Inquiry Skill Practice—Make a Model**

Draw a picture of the moon in each box to show how it looks different every seven days.

2. **Use Vocabulary**

Write the word *moon* in the sentence that tells about it.

The _____ is the center of the solar system.

The _____ is a huge ball of rock that moves in an orbit around Earth.

© Harcourt

Name _____

3. (Focus Skill) Cause and Effect

Use this chart with the Lesson Review.

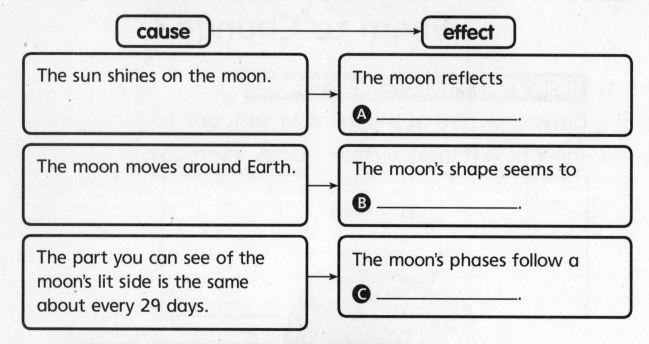

cause → effect

The sun shines on the moon. → The moon reflects **A** _____.

The moon moves around Earth. → The moon's shape seems to **B** _____.

The part you can see of the moon's lit side is the same about every 29 days. → The moon's phases follow a **C** _____.

4. Critical Thinking and Problem Solving

Suppose the moon in the sky looked like the moon in the picture below.

About how many days would it take for the moon to look like this again? How do you know?

_____

_____

_____

© Harcourt

Name _____

Date _____

Lesson 4 - What Causes the Seasons?

1. **Inquiry Skill Practice–Communicate**

Communicate how you know that North America is having winter.

_____

_____

2. **Use Vocabulary**

Match the word to the words that tell about it.

• a time of year that has a certain kind of weather

season •

• the time it takes the moon to orbit Earth

• the time it takes Earth to rotate around the sun

© Harcourt

Name _____

3. ⭐Focus Skill Cause and Effect

Use this chart with the Lesson Review.

cause   **effect**

| Part of Earth is tilted toward the sun. | → | That part has summer. Temperatures are **A** _____. There are **B** _____ hours of daylight. |

| Part of Earth is tilted away from the sun. | → | That part has **C** _____. Temperatures are **D** _____. There are **E** _____ hours of daylight. |

4. Critical Thinking and Problem Solving

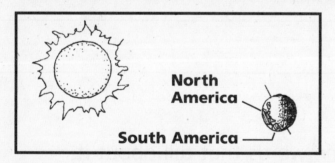

Why does North America have summer when
South America has winter?

_____

_____

© Harcourt

Name _____

Date _____

Write a Letter About Juice Pops

Write to Express–Friendly Letter

Write a letter to a friend about how you make juice pops. In your letter, tell what you mix together to make juice pops. Tell how these things are changed when juice pops are prepared. Use the letter format below to help you plan your letter.

Heading

Today's date:

Greeting

Dear _____,

Body of letter

First paragraph (What you use to make juice pops):

Second Paragraph (What changes when you make juice pops):

Closing

Your friend,

_____

© Harcourt

Name _____

Date _____

Observing and Classifying Matter

Look at each word puzzle. Think about why the
words go together.

rough — smooth	white — snow	ruler — tool
wet — dry	green — grass	bear — animal

Rough and smooth are opposites. Why does wet go with dry?
White is the color of snow. Why does green go with grass?
A ruler is a kind of tool. Why does bear go with animal?

Look at each word puzzle below. How do the first two words
go together? Write the word that goes with the third word
in the same way. Use words from the box.

gas	liquid	texture	solid	mass	volume

1. wood — solid
juice — _____

4. red — color
smooth — _____

2. centimeter — length
milliliter — _____

5. meterstick — length
balance — _____

3. water — liquid
air — _____

6. round — shape
soft — _____

Name _____

Date _____

Lesson 1 - What Is Matter?

1. **Inquiry Skill Practice–Compare**

Label each picture a solid, a liquid, or a gas.
How are they alike and different?

_____   _____   _____

_____

_____

2. **Use Vocabulary**

Write the word that best completes each sentence.

matter	property	mass

Everything is made up of _____.

How much matter something has is its _____.

The color or shape of something is a _____.

Name _____

3. (Focus Skill) Compare and Contrast

Use this chart with the Lesson Review.

Matter

alike

All matter takes

up **A** _____ .

All matter has

B _____ .

different

Matter can be a solid,

a **C** _____ ,

or a **D** _____ .

4. Critical Thinking and Problem Solving

If the hidden object has the same properties as the airplane, what can you tell about the hidden object?

_____

_____

_____

_____

© Harcourt

Name _____

Date _____

Lesson 2 - What Are Solids?

1. **Inquiry Skill Practice–Measure**

Each picture shows a balance with an object and a mass. The mass is the same on each balance. Number the pictures to show the order of the objects from least mass to most mass.

_____   _____   _____

2. **Use Vocabulary**

Write the word that best completes each sentence.

solid	texture	centimeter

Glass has a smooth _____.

A _____ is a unit used to measure length.

A _____ has its own shape.

Name _____

3. (Focus Skill) **Compare and Contrast**

Use this chart with the Lesson Review.

> **Solids**

alike   **different**

All solids have

A _____.

All solids take up

B _____.

All solids have their own

C _____.

Solids can be different colors,

sizes, and **D** _____.

Some solids are hard, and

some are **E** _____.

Solids can have
different textures.

4. **Critical Thinking and Problem Solving**

The clay, wood, and twig are solid matter. What can
you tell about the shapes of solids by looking at them?

_____

_____

_____

Name _____

Date _____

Lesson 3 - What Are Liquids?

1. **Inquiry Skill Practice–Infer**

Observe the pictures. What can you infer?

_____

_____

_____

2. **Use Vocabulary**

Match the word to the words that tell about

it.

liquid •   • how much space a liquid
                                          takes up

milliliter •   • matter you can pour that
                                          does not have its own shape

volume •   • a unit used to measure the
                                          volume of a liquid

Name _____

3. (Focus Skill) Main Idea and Details

Use this chart with the Lesson Review.

Main Idea and Details

Liquids are a form of matter.

A liquid has	It takes up	It does not have its own	You can measure it to find its
Ⓐ _____.	Ⓑ _____.	Ⓒ _____.	Ⓓ _____.

4. Critical Thinking and Problem Solving

Why do liquids always need to be kept in a container?

_____

_____

© Harcourt

Lesson 4 - What Are Gases?

1. **Inquiry Skill Practice—Infer**

How does the tire in each picture look different?

_____

_____

What can you infer about air from these pictures?

_____

2. **Use Vocabulary**

Match the word to the picture that shows its meaning.

gas •

© Harcourt

Name _____

3. ⭐(Focus Skill) **Main Idea and Details**

Use this chart with the Lesson Review.

Main Idea and Details

Gases are a form of matter.

| A gas takes up Ⓐ _____. | It has Ⓑ _____. | It Ⓒ _____ all the space of its container. | You often cannot Ⓓ _____ it. |

4. **Critical Thinking and Problem Solving**

How could you use a beach ball to show a friend that air is a gas that takes up space and has mass?

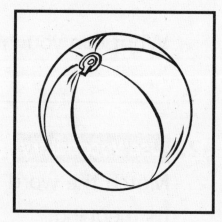

_____

_____

_____

_____

Name _____

Date _____

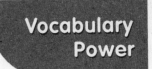

Changes in Matter

When you see a new word, look for parts you know.
They can help you figure out the meaning of the word.

What does <u>burnt</u> mean?
You know that <u>burn</u> means to change matter with heat or
fire. So <u>burnt</u> might have to do with heat changing matter.

Use word parts to figure out the new words below.

1. To <u>mix</u> is to blend together. A **<u>mixer</u>** is a tool
that helps blend things together. Circle other
words that have to do with blending together.

remix	**mixture**	**Mexico**	**fixture**	**unmixed**

2. <u>Vapor</u> is a kind of matter in the air. **Water
<u>vapor</u>** is water in the air. Circle other words
that tell about matter in the air.

vacuum	**vaporizer**	**evaporation**	**envelope**	**viper**

© Harcourt

Name _____

Date _____

Lesson 1 - How Can Matter Change?

1. **Inquiry Skill Practice–Communicate**

One picture shows vegetables.
The other shows a salad.
Communicate how the
vegetables changed when they
were made into a salad.

_____

_____

2. **Use Vocabulary**

Match the word to the picture that shows
its meaning.

mixture •

© Harcourt

Name _____

3. 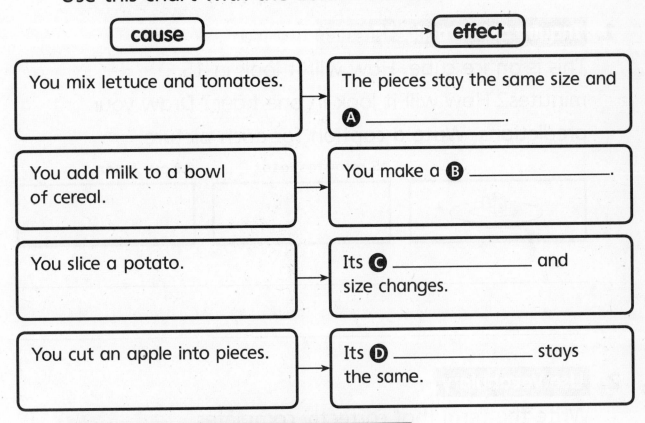 Cause and Effect

Use this chart with the Lesson Review.

cause	→	effect
You mix lettuce and tomatoes.	→	The pieces stay the same size and Ⓐ _____.
You add milk to a bowl of cereal.	→	You make a Ⓑ _____.
You slice a potato.	→	Its Ⓒ _____ and size changes.
You cut an apple into pieces.	→	Its Ⓓ _____ stays the same.

4. Critical Thinking and Problem Solving

These two loaves of bread were exactly the same. Then one was sliced. Did that change its shape, its mass, or both? How could a balance help you find the answer?

_____

_____

Name _____

Date _____

Lesson 2 - How Can Water Change?

1. Inquiry Skill Practice–Predict

This is an ice cube. How will it look in 15 minutes? How will it look in one hour? Draw your predictions. Write a caption for each picture.

	15 minutes later	**1 hour later**

_____ _____ _____

_____ _____ _____

2. Use Vocabulary

Write the term that correctly completes each sentence.

condensation evaporation water vapor

Water that has changed to a gas is called

_____.

The change from a liquid to a gas is called

_____.

The change from a gas to a liquid is called

_____.

© Harcourt

Name _____

3. (Focus Skill) **Cause and Effect**

Use this chart with the Lesson Review.

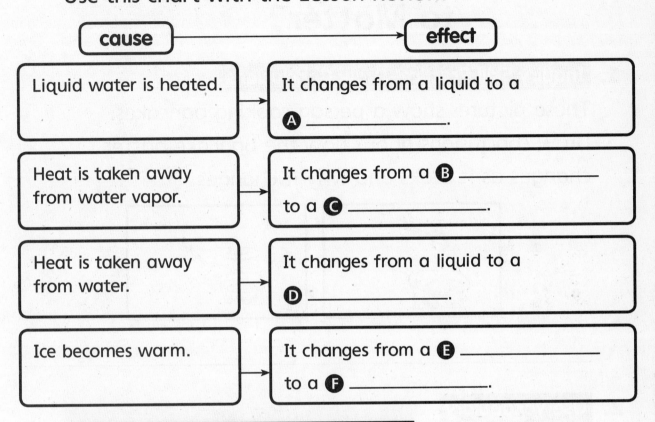

cause → effect

Liquid water is heated.	It changes from a liquid to a A _____.
Heat is taken away from water vapor.	It changes from a B _____ to a C _____.
Heat is taken away from water.	It changes from a liquid to a D _____.
Ice becomes warm.	It changes from a E _____ to a F _____.

4. **Critical Thinking and Problem Solving**

Does ice have more mass than liquid water?
How can you use a balance, a bowl of ice,
and masses to find out?

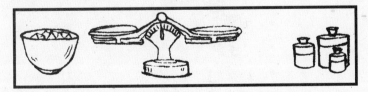

_____

_____

_____

© Harcourt

Name _____

Date _____

Lesson 3 - What Are Other Changes to Matter?

1. **Inquiry Skill Practice–Draw Conclusions**

These pictures show a person cooking pancakes. Draw conclusions about how the pancake batter changes as it cooks and why it changes.

2. **Use Vocabulary**

Match the word to the picture that shows its meaning. Write a sentence about the picture.

burning .

Name _____

3. (Focus Skill) Cause and Effect

Use this chart with the Lesson Review.

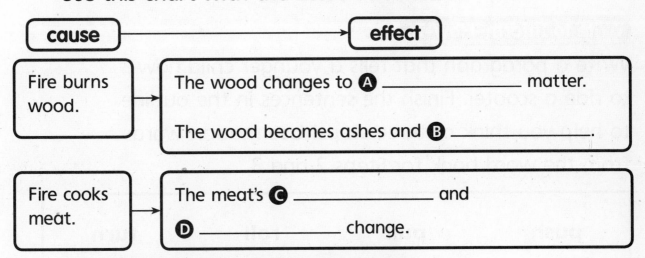

cause ————————————————→ effect

Fire burns wood.

→ The wood changes to **A** _____ matter.

The wood becomes ashes and **B** _____.

Fire cooks meat.

→ The meat's **C** _____ and

D _____ change.

4. Critical Thinking and Problem Solving

How does a pizza change as it cooks?

_____

_____

_____

Name _____

Date _____

Tell How to Ride a Scooter

Write to Inform–How-To

Write a paragraph that tells a younger child how to ride a scooter. Finish the sentences in the outline to help you think of three steps. Use motion words from the word bank for Steps 2 and 3.

| push | pull | roll | turn |

Step 1

Start with one foot . . .

Step 2

Move forward by . . .

Step 3

To change direction, . . .

© Harcourt

Light and Heat

Some words can be used in more than one way. Look at the underlined words here.

The bell <u>sounds</u> at noon each day.
I like the <u>sounds</u> of birds in the trees.

Each word in the box can be used in more than one way. Complete each sentence pair with a word from the box.

heat	light	energy

1. The oven gives off a lot of _____.
   Remember to _____ your soup before you eat it.

2. Big trucks use more _____ than small cars.
   I had enough _____ to rake the whole yard.

3. The sun gives off a bright _____.
   Bill's mom will _____ the campfire.

Lesson 1 - What Is Energy?

1. **Inquiry Skill Practice–Plan an Investigation**

Plan the fastest way to change
an ice cube into water. Draw the
ice where you would put it in
the picture.

Communicate what you would do and why.

_____

_____

_____

2. **Use Vocabulary**

Match each word to the sentence that tells about it.

energy • • It is the energy you use when you
      plug something into an outlet.

heat • • It is energy from the sun.

light • • It has different forms and can cause
      matter to move.

electricity • • It is energy that makes things warmer.

solar energy • • It is energy that lets you see.

© Harcourt

Name _____

3. ⭐(Focus Skill) Main Idea and Details

Use this chart with the Lesson Review.

Main Idea and Details

> Energy is something that can cause matter to move or change.

Three forms of energy are heat, **A** _____, and **B** _____.	Energy can come from the sun, wind, and moving **C** _____.	Energy can also come from gasoline and other **D** _____.

4. Critical Thinking and Problem Solving

Each thing listed below uses electricity. Then it changes the electricity into one or more other forms of energy. Write the name or names of these forms of energy on the line.

toaster   _____

radio   _____

iron   _____

television   _____

lamp   _____

© Harcourt

Name _____

Date _____

Lesson 2 - What Is Light?

1. **Inquiry Skill Practice–Draw Conclusions**

Observe carefully. Use your observations
and what you know to draw conclusions
about how light is moving in
this picture.

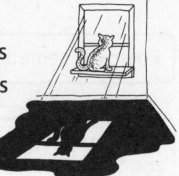

_____

_____

_____

2. **Use Vocabulary**

Write the word *reflect* below the picture that
shows its meaning.

_____   _____   _____

© Harcourt

Name _____

3. ⭐ **Focus Skill** | **Main Idea and Details**

Use this chart with the Lesson Review.

Main Idea and Details

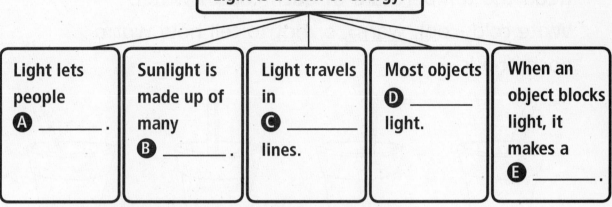

Light is a form of energy.

| Light lets people **A** _____ . | Sunlight is made up of many **B** _____ . | Light travels in **C** _____ lines. | Most objects **D** _____ light. | When an object blocks light, it makes a **E** _____ . |

4. | **Critical Thinking and Problem Solving**

How is the ball in this picture like light? Tell why and give an example.

_____

_____

_____

© Harcourt

Name _____

Date _____

Lesson 3 - What Is Heat?

1. **Inquiry Skill Practice–Measure**

Read the temperature of each cup of water.
Write <u>cold</u>, <u>cool</u>, <u>warm</u>, or <u>hot</u> to tell how warm
each one is.

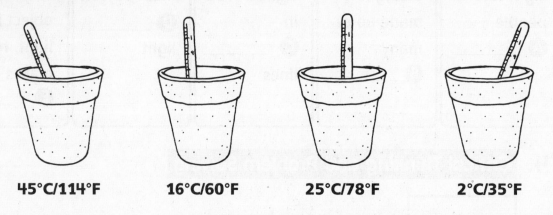

45°C/114°F   16°C/60°F   25°C/78°F   2°C/35°F

_____   _____   _____   _____

2. **Use Vocabulary**

Write the word from the box that best
completes each sentence.

thermometer	temperature	friction

When you rub your hands together, they feel warmer

because of _____.

You can measure how warm something is with

a _____.

Something that is cold has a low _____.

© Harcourt

Name _____

3. (Focus Skill) Main Idea and Details

Use this chart with the Lesson Review.

Main Idea and Details

```
┌─────────────────────────────────────────────────────┐
│   Heat is a form of energy that makes things warmer. │
└─────────────────────────────────────────────────────┘
```

| Objects produce heat when they **A** _____ against each other. | People produce heat when they **B** _____ fuel. | Energy stations use heat to produce **C** _____. | Heat moves from warmer objects to **D** _____ ones. |

4. Critical Thinking and Problem Solving

Some pots and pans have wooden or plastic handles. Do you think this is a good feature? Why or why not?

_____

_____

Name _____

Date _____

Sound

Look at these sentences. Each one includes two words that are opposites. The opposites tell about the word in bold.

A **bell** can be <u>big</u> or <u>small</u>.

A **song** can be <u>long</u> or <u>short</u>.

Now look at the words below. Write opposites to complete the sentences. Use the words in the box.

quickly	short	loud	high
long	soft	slowly	low

1. A **sound wave** can travel a _____ or _____ distance.

2. A sound's **pitch** can be _____ or _____.

3. The **loudness** of a sound can be _____ or _____.

4. A string can **vibrate** _____ or _____ to make sound.

© Harcourt

Name _____

Date _____

Lesson 1 - What Causes Sound?

1. **Inquiry Skill Practice—Communicate**

Look at these pictures and communicate
about the kind of sound each object makes.
What causes all the sounds?

_____

_____

_____

2. **Use Vocabulary**

Write the word that best completes
each sentence.

sound	vibrate

When things _____, they move quickly back
and forth.

_____ is energy that you can hear.

© Harcourt

Name _____

3. (Focus Skill) Cause and Effect

Use this chart with the Lesson Review.

| cause | → | effect |

Something vibrates.	→	You hear **A** _____.
Something stops vibrating.	→	The sound **B** _____.
Vibrations move through the ear.	→	The eardrum **C** _____.

4. Critical Thinking and Problem Solving

You can hear the sound a guitar makes when you pluck its strings. Why does the sound stop after a short time?

_____

_____

_____

© Harcourt

Name _____

Date _____

Lesson 2 - How Does Sound Travel?

1. **Inquiry Skill Practice–Predict**

Sound can travel through solids, liquids, and gases. Predict what kinds of matter the sound of the knock will travel through to reach the person.

_____

_____

_____

2. **Use Vocabulary**

Match the words to the words that tell about them.

• water that makes noise

sound wave • • a very loud sound

• vibrations moving through matter

Name _____

3.  Main Idea and Details

Use this chart with the Lesson Review.

Main Idea and Details

Sound travels through different kinds of matter.

| Sound can travel through air, which is a **A** _____. | Dolphins make sounds that travel through water, a **B** _____. | Sound travels through **C** _____, such as wood and glass. |

4. Critical Thinking and Problem Solving

Why can the people standing behind the marching band hear its music?

_____

_____

© Harcourt

Name _____

Date _____

Lesson 3 - How Do We Make Different Sounds?

1. **Inquiry Skill Practice–Hypothesize**

Hypothesize how the rubber-band instruments will sound different.

_____

_____

2. **Use Vocabulary**

Match the word to the words that tell about it.

loudness •   • how near or far a sound is

pitch •   • how high or low a sound is

                                  • how loud or soft a sound is

© Harcourt

Name _____

3. 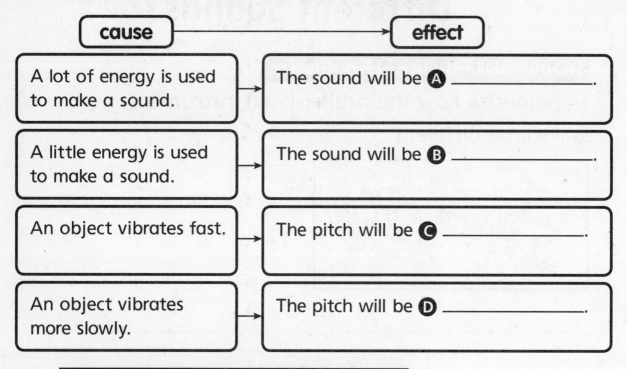 **Cause and Effect**

Use this chart with the Lesson Review.

cause	→	effect
A lot of energy is used to make a sound.	→	The sound will be **A** _____.
A little energy is used to make a sound.	→	The sound will be **B** _____.
An object vibrates fast.	→	The pitch will be **C** _____.
An object vibrates more slowly.	→	The pitch will be **D** _____.

4. **Critical Thinking and Problem Solving**

Which teacher is using more energy to speak?

_____

_____

_____

Motion

Look at these words. How do they change when you add word endings?

magnet + –<u>ic</u> = magnet<u>ic</u> acid + –<u>ic</u> = acid<u>ic</u>	observe + –<u>ant</u> = observ<u>ant</u> repel + –<u>ant</u> = repell<u>ant</u>

Now look at the words below. Add the new ending to each one to make a new word. Then use what you know to give the new word's meaning.

1. force + –<u>ful</u> = _____

Circle the letter next to the new word's meaning.

A with no force

B with a lot of force

2. motion + –<u>less</u> = _____

Circle the letter next to the new word's meaning.

A moving a lot

B not moving

3. speed + –<u>y</u> = _____

Circle the letter next to the new word's meaning.

A with no speed

B with a lot of speed

© Harcourt

Name _____

Date _____

Lesson 1 - What Are Ways Things Move?

1. **Inquiry Skill Practice–Plan an Investigation**

Look at these pictures. Use the items to plan an investigation to find out which ways the toy car can move.

Step 1: _____

Step 2: _____

Step 3: _____

2. **Use Vocabulary**

Write the word that best completes each sentence.

motion	speed

When something moves, it is in _____.

_____ is how fast something moves.

© Harcourt

Name _____

3. **Main Idea and Details**

Use this chart with the Lesson Review.

Main Idea and Details

Objects can move in different paths and at different speeds.

| A toy car can move in a straight line. | A swing moves **A** _____ . | The hands of a clock move in a **B** _____ . | Objects can move quickly or **C** _____ . |

4. **Critical Thinking and Problem Solving**

If you are watching two people walk, how can you tell which one is walking faster?

_____

_____

_____

Name _____

Date _____

Lesson 2 - What Makes Things Move?

1. **Inquiry Skill Practice–Classify**

Look at the pictures. Classify the movements as pushes or pulls. Mark an **X** in the correct box.

movement	push	pull
hitting a baseball		
opening a door		

2. **Use Vocabulary**

Match the word to the words that tell about it.

force •

• a simple machine that makes moving or lifting things easier

lever •

• a force that pulls things toward the center of Earth

gravity •

• a force that slows down or stops moving things

inclined plane •

• a push or pull that causes something to move

friction •

• a simple machine made up of a bar that pivots, or turns, on a fixed point

Name _____

3. (Focus Skill) **Cause and Effect**

Use this chart with the Lesson Review.

cause   effect

cause	effect
An object is pushed or **Ⓐ** _____.	→ The object moves.
Ⓑ _____ pulls an object.	→ The object moves toward Earth.
Two objects rub against each other and cause **Ⓒ** _____.	→ Moving objects slow down or stop.

4. **Critical Thinking and Problem Solving**

Why is it easier for the first child to skate faster?

_____

_____

_____

© Harcourt

Name _____

Date _____

Lesson 3 - How Do Magnets Move Things?

1. **Inquiry Skill Practice–Hypothesize**

Look at the pictures. Hypothesize which object the magnet will attract. Explain why.

mitten   **glass of water**   **key**

_____

_____

2. **Use Vocabulary**

Write the word that best completes each sentence.

The two **N** poles on different magnets _____ each other.

All magnets have two _____.

Opposite poles on a magnet _____ each other.

A _____ can push or pull things made of iron or steel.

| magnet |
| poles |
| attract |
| repel |

© Harcourt

Name _____

3. **Main Idea and Details**

Use this chart with the Lesson Review.

Main Idea and Details

> **Magnets can pull iron or steel. Magnets can push and pull other magnets.**

A magnet has an N pole and an **A** _____ pole.	Opposite poles **B** _____ each other.	The same poles on different magnets **C** _____ each other.	A magnet's force can move through air, water, and some **D** _____.

4. **Critical Thinking and Problem Solving**

Suppose you have two toy cars. You can pull the first car with a magnet but not the second one. What can you infer about the two cars?

_____

_____

_____

References

Contents

Identify the Main Idea and Details

Learning how to find the main idea can help you understand what you read. The main idea of a paragraph is what it is mostly about. The details tell you more about it. Read this paragraph.

Snakes swallow their food whole. They cannot chew their food. Snakes' mouths are flexible. They can open their mouths very wide. They can move their jaws from side to side. Their skin can stretch to help open their mouths wide. Because it can open its mouth wide, a snake can swallow a larger animal.

This chart shows the main idea and details.

Detail: Snakes cannot chew.	Detail: Snakes' mouths are flexible.

Main Idea Snakes must swallow their food whole.

Detail: Snakes' skin can stretch to help open their mouths wide.	Detail: Snakes can open their mouths very wide.

Compare and Contrast

Focus Skill

Learning how to compare and contrast can help you understand what you read. Comparing is finding what is alike. Contrasting is finding what is different. Read this paragraph.

The desert and the forest are both environments for living things. Many kinds of plants and animals live there. But the desert is dry for most of the year. The forest has more rain. Plants such as cactuses live in the desert. Oak and maple trees live in the forest.

This chart shows comparing and contrasting.

Compare

alike
Both are environments.
Many kinds of plants and animals live in each environment.

Contrast

different
Deserts are dry.
Forests have more rain.
Plants such as cactuses live in the desert.
Oak and maple trees live in the forest.

Cause and Effect

Learning how to find cause and effect can help you understand what you read. A cause is why something happens. An effect is what happens. Some paragraphs have more than one cause or effect. Read this paragraph.

People once used a poison called DDT to get rid of pests. Small birds eat bugs. Some large birds eat small birds. When small birds ate bugs sprayed with DDT, the DDT got into their bodies. When large birds ate small birds, the DDT got into their bodies, too. DDT caused birds to lay eggs that broke easily.

This chart shows cause and effect.

Cause

Small birds ate bugs sprayed with DDT.

Effects

Large birds that ate small birds got DDT into their bodies. The DDT made the birds lay eggs that broke easily.

Sequence

Focus Skill

Learning how to find sequence can help you understand what you read. Sequence is the order in which something happens. Some paragraphs use words that help you understand order. Read this paragraph. Look at the underlined words.

Ricky and his grandpa made a special dessert. <u>First</u>, Grandpa peeled apples and cut them into small chunks. <u>Next</u>, Ricky put the apple chunks and some raisins in a bowl. <u>Then</u>, Grandpa put the bowl into a microwave oven for about ten minutes. <u>Last</u>, when the bowl was cool enough to touch, Ricky and Grandpa ate their dessert.

This chart shows sequence.

1. <u>First</u>, Grandpa peeled apples and cut them into chunks.

2. <u>Next</u>, Ricky put apple chunks and raisins in a bowl.

3. <u>Then</u>, Grandpa put the bowl in a microwave oven for ten minutes.

4. <u>Last</u>, Ricky and Grandpa ate their dessert.

Draw Conclusions

When you draw conclusions, you tell what you have learned. What you learned also includes your own ideas. Read this paragraph.

The body coverings of many animals can help them hide. One kind of moth has wings with a pattern that looks like tree bark. The moth is hard to see when it is resting on a tree. A polar bear's white coat can make it hard to see in the snow. Being hard to see can help protect an animal or help it hunt other animals.

This chart shows how to draw conclusions.

What I Read

The body coverings of a moth and a polar bear can help them hide.

What I Know

I have seen an insect that looks like a leaf. The insect was very hard to see when it was on a tree branch.

Conclusion

Some animals that live near my own home have body coverings that help them hide.

Summarize

When you summarize, you tell the main idea and details you remember from what you read. Read this paragraph.

> The leaves of a tree grow in the summer. They provide food for the growing tree. Leaves trap energy from the sun. They get water from the ground. They take in gases from the air. Leaves use these things to make food for the tree.

This chart shows how to summarize.

Recall Detail Leaves grow in the summer	**Recall Detail** Leaves trap sunlight	**Recall Detail** Leaves collect water from the ground and gases from the air.

Summary   Leaves use sunlight, water, and gases to make food for the tree.

Using Tables, Charts, and Graphs

Gather Data

When you investigate in science, you need to collect data.

Suppose you want to find out what kinds of things are in soil. You can sort the things you find into groups.

Things I Found in One Cup of Soil

Parts of Plants   Small Rocks   Parts of Animals

By studying the circles, you can see the different items found in soil. However, you might display the data in a different way. For example, you could use a tally table.

Reading a Tally Table

You can show your data in a tally table.

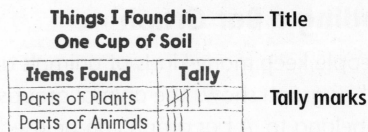

Things I Found in ——— Title
One Cup of Soil

Items Found	Tally
Parts of Plants	⊥⊦⊦⊦ I
Parts of Animals	III
Small Rocks	⊥⊦⊦⊦ II

Tally marks

Data

How to Read a Tally Table

1. **Read** the tally table. Use the labels.

2. **Study** the data.

3. **Count** the tally marks.

4. **Draw conclusions**. Ask yourself questions like the ones on this page.

Skills Practice

1. How many parts of plants were found in the soil?

2. How many more small rocks were found in the soil than parts of animals?

3. How many parts of plants and parts of animals were found?

Using Tables, Charts, and Graphs

Reading a Bar Graph

People keep many kinds of animals as pets. This bar graph shows the animal groups most pets belong to. A bar graph can be used to compare data.

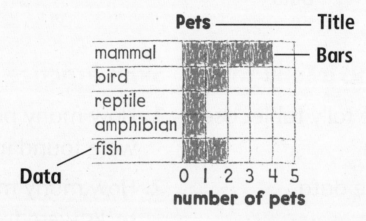

How to Read a Bar Graph

1. **Look** at the title to learn what kind of information is shown.

2. **Read** the graph. Use the labels.

3. **Study** the data. Compare the bars.

4. **Draw conclusions**. Ask yourself questions like the ones on this page.

Skills Practice

1. How many pets are mammals?

2. How many pets are birds?

3. How many more pets are mammals than fish?

Reading a Picture Graph

Some second-grade students were asked to choose their favorite season. They made a picture graph to show the results. A picture graph uses pictures to show information.

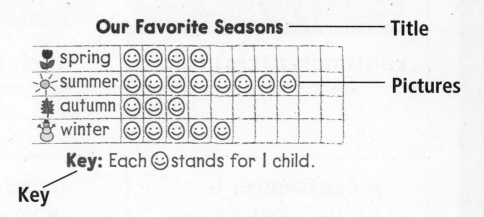

Our Favorite Seasons ——————— Title

Pictures

Key: Each ☺ stands for I child.

Key

How to Read a Picture Graph

1. **Look** at the title to learn what kind of information is shown.

2. **Read** the graph. Use the labels.

3. **Study** the data. Compare the number of pictures in each row.

4. **Draw conclusions**. Ask yourself questions like the ones on this page.

Skills Practice

1. Which season did the most students choose?

2. Which season did the fewest students choose?

3. How many students in all chose summer or winter?

Measurements

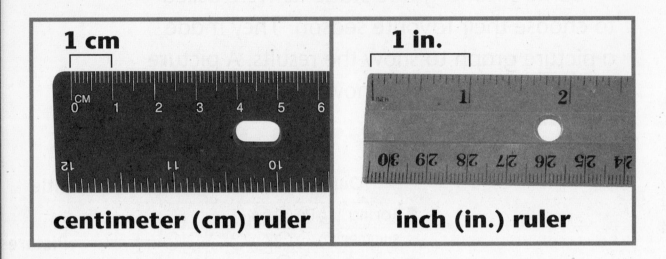

1 cm

CM
0 1 2 3 4 5 6

12 11 10

centimeter (cm) ruler

1 in.

INCH 1 2

30 29 28 27 26 25 24

inch (in.) ruler

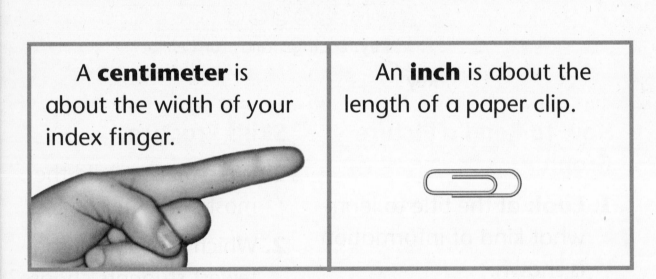

A **centimeter** is about the width of your index finger.

An **inch** is about the length of a paper clip.

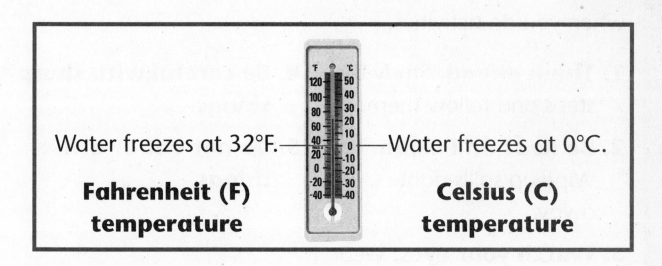

Water freezes at 32°F. — **Fahrenheit (F) temperature** — Water freezes at 0°C. **Celsius (C) temperature**

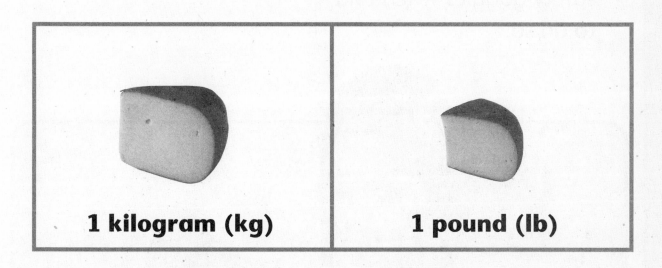

1 kilogram (kg)

1 pound (lb)

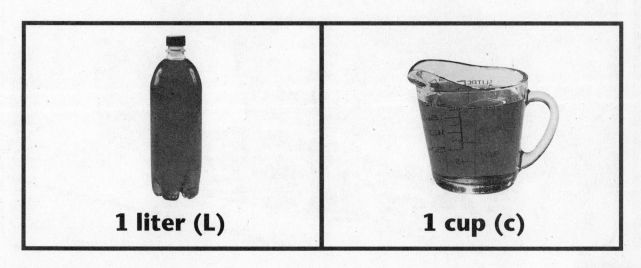

1 liter (L)

1 cup (c)

Safety in Science

Here are some safety rules to follow when you do activities.

1. **Think ahead.** Study the steps and follow them.

2. **Be neat and clean.** Wipe up spills right away.

3. **Watch your eyes.** Wear safety goggles when told to do so.

4. **Be careful with sharp things.**

5. **Do not eat or drink things.**

VOCABULARY GAMES
and CARDS

Contents

© Harcourt

Vocabulary Games

You can use the word cards on pages RS123–RS179 to play these games.

Which One Does Not Fit?

You will need word cards

Grouping whole class, large group, or pairs

1. Choose three word cards. Two of them should fit a category. One of them should not fit that group.

2. Ask other players, "Which card does not fit?" Choose one player to tell why the word card does not fit the group.

3. Take turns putting word cards into groups. Guess which word card does not fit each group.

Word-O!

You will need 12 word cards for each player,
12 word cards for the caller

Grouping whole class, large group, or small group

1. Make three rows with your word cards. Each row should have three words in it. Place the words in any order face up. You should have three words that you do not use.

2. The caller will call one word at a time. If one of your words is called, turn it over.

3. When you have three words in a row turned over, you have won! Call out, "Word-O!"

ABC Ladder

You will need word cards

Grouping partners or small group

1. Place all of the word cards face up so that you can read each word.

2. Start making the ladder. Place the word card that comes first in ABC order.

3. Which word will come next in ABC order? Place it above the first word to form the ladder.

4. Take turns. Add word cards until all of them are placed in ABC order.

adapt

amphibian

attract

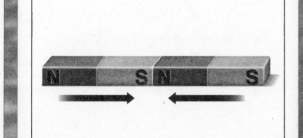

bird

© Harcourt

amphibian

[am•FIB•ee•uhn]

The group of animals with smooth, wet skin. Young amphibians live in the water, and most adults live on land.

2

adapt

[uh•DAPT]

To change. Animals and plants adapt over time to live in their environments.

1

bird

[BERD]

The group of animals with feathers on their bodies and wings. Most birds can fly.

4

attract

[uh•TRAKT]

To pull something. Opposite poles of two magnets attract each other.

3

© Harcourt

boulder

5

burning

6

centimeter

7

condensation

8

burning

[BER•ning]

The change of a substance into ashes and smoke.

6

boulder

[BOHL•der]

A very large rock.

5

condensation

[kahn•dhun•SAY•shuhn]

The change of water from a gas to a liquid. Condensation happens when heat is taken away from water vapor.

8

centimeter

[SEN•tuh•mee•ter]

A unit used to measure how long a solid is. Centimeters are marked on many rulers.

7

© Harcourt

condense

9

constellation

10

desert

11

dinosaur

12

© Harcourt

constellation

[kahn•stuh•LAY•shuhn]

A group of stars that form a pattern.

10

condense

[kuhn•DENS]

To change from water vapor gas into liquid water. Water vapor condenses when heat is taken away.

9

dinosaur

[DY•nuh•sawr]

An animal that lived on Earth millions of years ago. Dinosaurs have become extinct.

12

desert

[DEZ•ert]

An environment that is very dry because it gets little rain.

11

© Harcourt

drought

13

earthquake

14

electricity

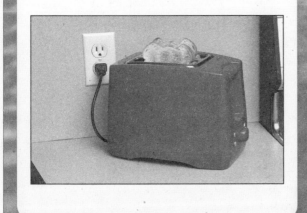

15

endangered

16

earthquake

[ERTH•kwayk]

A shaking of Earth's surface that can cause land to rise and fall.

drought

[DROWT]

A long time when it does not rain. During a drought the land may become dry, and plants may die.

endangered

[en•DAYN•jerd]

In danger of not being alive anymore. People can help endangered animals by protecting the places they live.

electricity

[uh•lek•TRIH•sih•tee]

A form of energy. People produce electricity by using energy from other sources.

© Harcourt

energy
17

environment
18

erosion
19

evaporate
20

environment

[en•vy•ruhn•muhnt]

All the living and nonliving things in a place.

18

energy

[EN•er•jee]

Something that can cause matter to move or change. Heat, light, and sound are forms of energy.

17

evaporate

[ee•VAP•uh•rayt]

To change from liquid water into a gas. Water evaporates when heat is added.

20

erosion

[uh•ROH•zhuhn]

A kind of change that happens when wind and water move sand and small rocks to a new place.

19

evaporation
21

extinct
22

fish
23

flowers
24

extinct

[ek•STINGT]

No longer living. Dinosaurs are extinct because none of them lives anymore.

22

evaporation

[ee•vap•uh•RAY•shuhn]

The change of water from a liquid to a gas. Evaporation happens when heat is added to liquid water.

21

flowers

[FLOW•erz]

The plant parts that help a plant make new plants. Part of the flower makes seeds that grow into new plants.

24

fish

[FISH]

The group of animals that live in water and get oxygen through gills. Fish have scales and use fins to swim.

23

food chain

(25)

food web

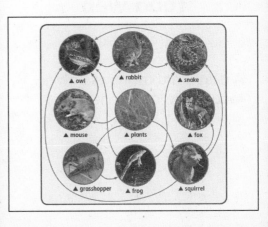

▲ owl ▲ rabbit ▲ snake
▲ mouse ▲ plants ▲ fox
▲ grasshopper ▲ frog ▲ squirrel

(26)

force

(27)

fossil

(28)

food web

[FOOD WEB]

A diagram that shows how food chains are connected.

26

food chain

[FOOD CHAYN]

A diagram that shows the order in which animals eat other living things.

25

fossil

[FAHS•uhl]

What is left of an animal or plant that lived long ago. A fossil can be a print in a rock or bones that have turned to rock.

28

force

[FAWRS]

A push or pull that makes something move. Magnetism is one kind of force.

27

© Harcourt

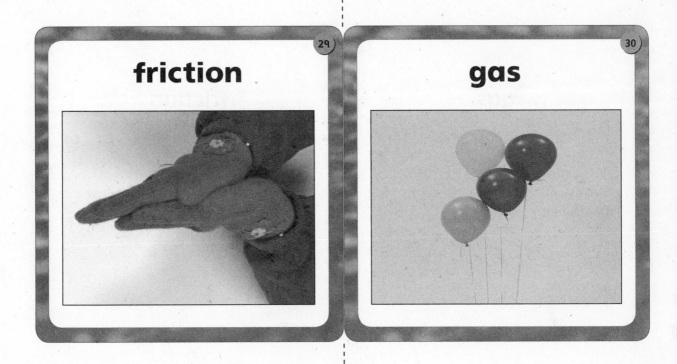

friction (29)

gas (30)

germinate (31)

grassland (32)

gas

[GAS]

The only form of matter that always fills all the space of its container.

30

friction

[FRIK•shuhn]

A force that slows down objects when they rub against each other. Friction also causes the objects to get warmer.

29

grassland

[GRAS•land]

An open environment covered with grass.

32

germinate

[JER•muh•nayt]

To start to grow. A seed may germinate when it gets water, warmth, and oxygen.

31

gravity

33

habitat

34

heat

35

inclined plane

36

habitat

[HAB•ih•tat]

A place where a living thing has the food, water, and shelter it needs to live.

34

gravity

[GRAV•ih•tee]

A force that pulls things toward the center of Earth.

33

inclined plane

[in•KLYND PLAYN]

A simple machine that makes moving or lifting things easier.

36

heat

[HEET]

Energy that makes things warmer. Heat can be used to cook food or melt things.

35

inquiry skills

37

investigate

38

leaves

39

lever

40

© Harcourt

investigate

[in•ves•tuh•gayt]

To plan and do a test. Scientists investigate to answer a question.

38

inquiry skills

[in•kwer•ee skilz]

A set of skills people use to find out information.

37

lever

[lev•er]

A simple machine made up of a bar that pivots, or turns, on a fixed point.

40

leaves

[leevz]

The parts of a plant that make food for the plant. Leaves use light, oxygen, and water to make food.

39

© Harcourt

life cycle
41

light
42

liquid
43

living
44

© Harcourt

light

[LYT]

A form of energy that lets you see. The sun and fires give off light energy.

42

life cycle

[LYF SY•kuhl]

All the stages of a plant's or an animal's life.

41

living

[LIV•ing]

Alive. Plants and animals are living things because they need food, water, and oxygen.

44

liquid

[LIK•wid]

A form of matter that takes the shape of its container.

43

© Harcourt

loudness

45

magnet

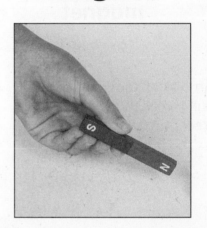

46

mammal

47

mass

48

magnet

[MAG•nit]

An object that can push and pull things made of iron and steel.

46

loudness

[LOWD•nuhs]

How loud or soft a sound is.

45

mass

[MAS]

The amount of matter in an object. Mass can be measured using a tool called a balance.

48

mammal

[MAM•uhl]

The group of animals with hair or fur on their bodies.

47

matter

milliliter

mineral

mixture

milliliter

[MIL•ih•leet•er]

A unit used to measure the volume of a liquid. Milliliters are marked on many measuring cups.

50

matter

[MAT•er]

The material all things are made of. Matter can be a solid, a liquid, or a gas.

49

mixture

[MIKS•cher]

A mix of different kinds of matter. Substances in a mixture do not become other substances.

52

mineral

[MIN•er•uhl]

Solid matter found in nature that was never living. Rocks are usually made of many different minerals.

51

© Harcourt

moon
53

motion
54

natural resource
55

nonliving
56

motion

[MOH•shuhn]

Movement. When something moves, it is in motion.

54

moon

[MOON]

A huge ball of rock that orbits Earth. The moon takes almost one month to go all the way around Earth.

53

nonliving

[nahn•LIV•ing]

Not alive. Air, water, and rocks are nonliving.

56

natural resource

[NACH•er•uhl REE•sawrs]

Anything in nature people can use to meet their needs.

55

© Harcourt

nutrients
57

ocean
58

orbit
59

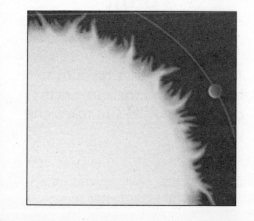

oxygen
60

ocean

[OH•shuhn]

A large body of salt water. Jellyfish and sharks live in oceans.

---

nutrients

[NOO•tree•uhnts]

Substances that plants and animals need to survive. Animals get nutrients from food. Plants get nutrients from the soil.

---

oxygen

[AHK•suh•juhn]

A gas in the air and water. Most living things need oxygen.

---

orbit

[AWR•bit]

The path a planet takes as it moves around the sun. Earth's orbit around the sun takes one year.

58

57

60

59

© Harcourt

pitch

61

planet

62

pole

63

pollution

64

planet

[PLAN•it]

A large ball of rock or gas that moves around the sun. Earth is our planet.

62

pitch

[PICH]

How high or low a sound is.

61

pollution

[puh•LOO•shuhn]

Waste that harms the air, water, or land.

64

pole

[POHL]

An end of a magnet. All magnets have a north-seeking pole and a south-seeking pole.

63

pond

65

precipitation

66

property

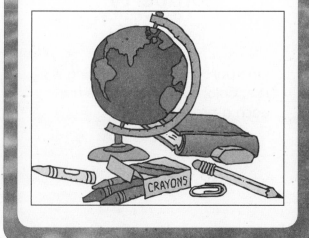

67

rain forest

68

© Harcourt

Vocabulary Cards

Reading Support and Homework

precipitation

[prih•sip•uh•TAY•shuhn]

Water that falls fom the sky. Rain, snow, sleet, and hail are kinds of precipitation.

66

pond

[PAHND]

A small, freshwater environment. Beavers and water lilies may live in a pond.

65

rain forest

[RAYN FAWR•ist]

An environment, with many tall trees, that gets rain almost every day.

68

property

[PRAH•per•tee]

One part of what something is like. Color, size, and shape are each a property.

67

recycle

reduce

reflect

repel

reduce

[ree•DOOS]

To use less of a resource.

(70)

recycle

[ree•SY•kuhl]

To use the materials in old things to make new things.

(69)

repel

[rih•PEL]

To push away. Poles that are the same on two magnets repel each other.

(72)

reflect

[rih•FLEKT]

To bounce off. Light reflects when it his most objects.

(71)

reptile

resource

reuse

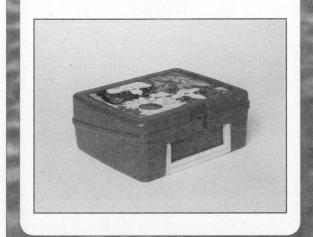

roots

resource

[REE•sawrs]

Anything people can use to meet their needs.

reptile

[REP•tyl]

The group of animals with dry skin covered in scales.

roots

[ROOTS]

The parts of a plant that take in water and nutrients. Most roots grow underground and help hold the plant in place.

reuse

[ree•YOOZ]

To use a resource again.

rotate

77

science tools

78

season

79

shelter

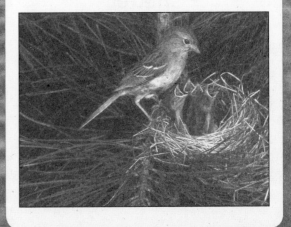

80

science tools

[SY•uhns TOOLZ]

Tools people use to find information.

78

rotate

[ROH•tayt]

To spin around like a top. Earth rotates one time every 24 hours.

77

shelter

[SHEL•ter]

A safe place to live. Birds may use a nest for shelter.

80

season

[SEE•zu

A time of year that has a certain kind of weather. The four seasons are spring, summer, fall, and winter.

79

shrub

81

soil

82

solar energy

83

solar system

84

© Harcourt

soil

[SOYL]

Bits of rocks mixed with matter that was once living.

82

shrub

[SHRUHB]

A bush. Shrubs have many woody stems.

81

solar system

[SOH•ler SIS•tuhm]

The sun, its planets, and other objects that move around the sun.

84

solar energy

[SOH•ler EN•er•jee]

Energy from the sun.

83

© Harcourt

solid

85

sound

86

sound wave

87

speed

88

sound

[SOWND]

Energy you can hear. Sounds are made when an object vibrates.

solid

[SAHL•id]

The only form of matter that has its own shape.

speed

[SPEED]

How fast something moves.

sound wave

[SOWND WAYV]

Vibrations moving through matter. When sound waves reach your ears, you can hear sound.

© Harcourt

star

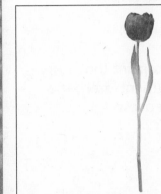

stems

survive

tadpole

stems

[STEMZ]

The parts of a plant that carry water and nutrients from the roots to the leaves.

90

star

[STAR]

A big ball of hot gases that give off light and heat energy. The sun is the closest star to Earth.

89

tadpole

[TAD•pohl]

A young frog. Tadpoles hatch from eggs and use gills to get oxygen from water.

92

survive

[ser•VYV]

To stay alive. Animals need food and water to survive.

91

© Harcourt

temperature

texture

thermometer

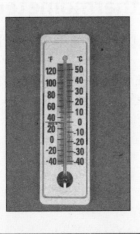

trunk

texture

[TEKS•cher]

The way something feels when you touch it.

94

temperature

[TEM•per•uh•cher]

A measure of how hot or cold something is.

93

trunk

[TRUHNK]

The one main stem of a tree.

96

thermometer

[ther•MAHM•uht•ter]

A tool that measures an object's temperature.

95

tundra 97

vibrate 98

volcano 99

volume 100

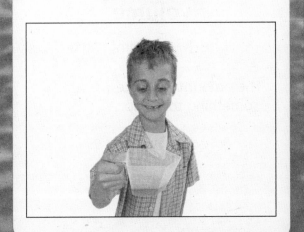

© Harcourt

vibrate

[VY•brayt]

To move back and forth quickly.

98

tundra

[TUHN•druh]

An environment that is cold and snowy. Plants that live in a tundra are short. The animals have think fur that helps them stay warm.

97

volume

[VAHL•yoom]

The amount of space something takes up.

100

volcano

[vahl•KAY•noh]

A place where hot melted rock called lava comes out of the ground onto Earth's surface.

99

© Harcourt

water cycle

101

water vapor

102

weather

103

weather pattern

104

water vapor

[WAWT•er VAY•per]

Water in the form of a gas.

102

water cycle

[WAW•ter SY•kuhl]

The movement of water from Earth's surface into the air and back to Earth's surface.

101

weather pattern

[WEH•ther PAT•ern]

A change in the weather that repeats.

104

weather

[WEH•ther]

What the air outside is like. The weather in summer is often sunny and hot.

103

© Harcourt

weathering

wind

wind

[WIND]

Air that is moving.

106

weathering

[WEH•ther•ing]

A kind of change that happens when wind and water break down rock into smaller pieces.

105

CURRICULUM